ravel

Bonnie Wai-Lee Kwong

NeoPoiesis Press, LLC

2775 Harbor Ave SW, Suite D, Seattle, WA 98126-2138
Inquiries: Info@NeoPoiesisPress.com
NeoPoiesisPress.com

Copyright © 2015 by Bonnie Wai-Lee Kwong

All rights reserved. No part of this book may be used or reproduced in any manner whatsoever without express written permission from the publisher except in the case of brief quotations embodied in critical articles and reviews.

Bonnie Wai-Lee Kwong – ravel
ISBN 978-0-9903565-3-0 (paperback : alk. paper)
    1. Poetry. I. Kwong, Bonnie Wai-Lee. II. ravel.

Library of Congress Control Number: 2015912669

First Edition

Cover Design: Milo Duffin and Stephen Roxborough

Printed in the United States of America.

for tomoko

Contents

Warp and Weft

Warp and Weft 7
To Swim Daily 10
The Journey of Goods 12
Pied Song 13
After Hours at the Convent School 14
Staircase 15
Sisters 16
The Parting of Hair 18
Mother 19
10,000 Thumbs 20
40 Chicken Eggs 21
The Monk and the Rifle 22
A House of Paper 24
Trade Winds 25
Fore and Aft 26
The Tint of Dawn 33
A Day in British Hong Kong 35
Summer at *Judgment* 37
All That She Wants 38
Landing 39
The Seal 41
The Boots and the Weary Bird 42

Cartographies

Cartographies	47
Half a Duet	50
Portrait of Winds	56
Where Indigo Meets Azure	60
Wishbone	61
Flotsam	62
Common Flower	64
Brooding	65
Letter from Sister to Brother	66
To Unborn Sons	67
Aspiration	68
Open Circles	69
California Rain Song	71
Paper Rain	75
Quotidian	76
The GI Bill	77
The Taste of Each	78
The Reader	81
The Tale	84
Contraband	89
The Experiment	102
The Way of Knots	105

Warp and Weft

Warp and Weft

There was no slack in the warp and weft
    my husband's great-grandma
        ran her fingers over.

A *burler* in a Rhode Island mill,
    her job was to feel
        for knots in the weave.

She wore her fingerprints away
    and her skin to such thinness
        blood might seep through.

Did the hours pass evenly
    in the rumble of the loom:
        again, again, gaining

in its appetite for cotton?
    Her father-in-law had returned
        from war and Confederate prison

to careless workers dropping scissors
    from the upper floors of the mill
        through slots where the driving belts ran.

The weave rent time after time.
    If that happens again I shall quit
        and never work in a mill....

It did, and he did,
    wrote his grandson,
        my husband's grandpa.

My father taught me a knot he'd learned
        as a boy, mending clothes
                when thread was scarce,

and he was left with only
        half an inch of thread
                between cloth and needle.

The needle couldn't flex,
        so he used the eye to lead the thread
                back through the loop, and tightened it.

Thread took no extensions,
        unlike the *iron thread* he salvaged
                on the streets of Wanchai

and soldered with rosin-scented flux.
        He cobbled together a radio
                where current flowed

through node and wire alike:
        threads of logic
                under music *cantabile*.

When my father first showed me
        a logical loop, I didn't
                follow the syntax.

For i = 0 to i <10
        i = i + 1
Next

I got the drift,
        as in the increment of age,
                the cycle of monsoons;

I like to study iteratives:
>from *crack* to *crackle*,   *drip* to *dribble*,
>>*wrest* to *wrestle*.

I condense the cacophonous words
>between my parents
>>into a single frequentative.

My father built circuits
>to turn speech into hexadecimals
>>my mother couldn't decipher.

For a living, I have learned to code
>in a language where objects
>>are discrete,

and strands
>of my mother's hair
>>are not allowed to enter.

There are burls in my logic,
>stray insects so small I can't feel
>>with my fingertips.

From a roving of discarded hair
>and insect wings, I weave
>>for my children to ravel.

To Swim Daily

is to wing one's way forward,
with each breath, to part water,
wave water behind.

My mother stood facing me
with outstretched hands, wading
backwards as I breathed my way toward her.
Waves bent light into tentacles on sand.
Her underwater body loomed large.

A refugee at six, my mother left no wake
from her boat for lovers or me to follow.
Where did she cross the divide
between Communist and colonial?
Not a porous line on a map,
but a solid wall of fear.

The summer after she landed,
she ran alone into the sea,
past the red flag on the beach.
The storm claimed her inflatable ring.
A stranger swept her ashore.
At the beach house, no one asked
if the girl who left was the wet one
who returned, or what she gave to the sea.

My mother once told me this story:
two lovers, champion swimmers
escaping the mainland,
cast farewells into the sea.
The man lagged.
The woman continued.

There are walls in the sea.

In the undertow of history,
we swim parallel to shore,
till the sea itself is tired.

The Journey of Goods

Hong Kong

A silk robe, continuous as water,
hangs light on a girl's shoulders,
one of many her grandfather
once bought to sell overseas.
All ships becalmed by war,
the robe never left the harbor.
After years in camphor,
it found its way to the girl,
her accidental inheritance.

Bedtime, her mother slips lobes
of knotted silk from their hoops,
buttons too tight for the girl's fingers.
She tells the girl silk is lighter than cotton.
She tells of the night she fled the mainland
for Hong Kong, how she waited her turn
at the docks, seventh child of the odd sex,
the weight of gold sewn into the lining
of her cotton jacket.

Knowing the viscous descent of gold in water,
she shifted her weight from one leg
      to the other, land to sea
                      to drifting land.

In the girl's dreams,
her mother undresses and plunges
into the sea, head above water,
shining scales below.

Pied Song

A leather blossom patches
a hole among stitched flowers
on my daughter's pants.
A scrape on my son's knee
scabs from the center.
Several of my mother's sisters
missing since childhood.
I sift yesterday's news
through mold and deckle,
press found feathers
and buds into the pulp.
The pied song of a mockingbird
cycles. My mother walks
uphill towards my children.
On my daughter's sun prints,
pale silhouettes blur into blue:
house key, leaf, absences.
My mother's forearms
are muscled with the weight
of the children she lifts.

After Hours at the Convent School

Hong Kong

Ours was a picture perfect
convent school, backdrop to
wedding photos strangers would take,
casting misty veils over bauhinia and azaleas,
cobblestones and bricks.

There were others
who occupied the negative space
only we the schoolgirls could see,
the way we sensed moisture in the air,
found moldy footprints on the wall,
beads of sweat on our chairs,

heard footsteps in the playground,
the click, clack of soldiers marching
spread through every hiding place. We knew
it wasn't morning dew in Mary's eyes,
seeping through her plastered face,
why waxen fingers still cleft layers
of new bark on the evergreen.

After hours, shuttlecocks whittled the air,
landed sometimes under the evergreen
we dared not touch, not even with rosaries
in our pockets and ten Hail Marys—
the evergreen so tall it could have been the one
a sister chose to hang herself in.
Was it after the soldiers left?

After hours, we gave each other history lessons,
without the facts, only the fear.

Staircase

Hong Kong

Against the slap-swish-slap of jump ropes
we recited the lesson of the old staircase:

never count the number of steps
as a schoolgirl once did, with each click
of heel on weathered wood, to 39.

The last step took her to a bonfire of books
in the hall, sisters in their habits walking
single file into flames, a slow ceremony
before the occupying soldiers.
The schoolgirl fainted.

She came to in a hospital, coaxed back
to the present from a fever, she was told.

I never asked the names of the immolated,
searched the hall for blackened floorboards,
or counted the steps on the old staircase.

It bore my weight as it did many before me,
and heaved under my breath
the song of an accordion.

Sisters

For Sister Rosemary of Maryknoll Convent School, Hong Kong

Fair daffodils, we weep to see
You haste away so soon
- Robert Herrick

Sister, so small, always stooping
as if to whisper in my ear,

you let me borrow English
books about skies blue as forget-me-nots

not found in Hong Kong,
where the sky itself is scarce.

My only references:
the opaque color of your eyes
the lavender print on your dress.

In your library, poetry was weeping
for *fair daffodils* I never knew,

the same flowers mother called narcissus,
sui seen 水仙, water nymphs rising from
swollen bulbs each Lunar New Year.

I never wept for *sui seen* 水仙,
though I relished the waiting, the final
release of sweetness in open air.

I thought all daffodils
had petals the color of crayon sun.

It took twelve years, another country:

El Salvador—four Maryknoll missionaries

raped and murdered by soldiers while
I learned to weep for *fair daffodils*

that haste away so soon,
not knowing their names were
Ita, Maura, Dorothy and Jean.

The Parting of Hair

Chinese University, Hong Kong

Approaching a lotus pond
on a narrow path, a student
heard a faint sobbing
                               above
the mating call of frogs, saw
a single braid
                 down the back
of a cotton blouse. A country girl
from the mainland, he thought.
Pressing
         a finger on her shoulder,
he asked why she was crying. Her back
to him, she told of
                a journey stolen
in a boxcar, how she and her lover crossed
the border
        in safety, and only
had to jump, how her lover landed
free, but her
         braid was caught
in the door of the moving train
that never stopped.
                 When he asked
to see her face, she turned to show
she had none
         but another braid
     in front.

Mother

No one knows where you came from,
only that you gave my father your eyes,
spread them open, set them like pearls
in his face. He wore them to school,
learned to write your name,
but not who you were:

perhaps his wet nurse, mother by trade,
your daughter a by-product cast aside.
Perhaps family servant, a barren wife
made to pay your way, a daughter
from an orphanage to your name.

When grandpa slapped cards
across the kitchen table, you conjured
coins from a neighbor's suds
to pay my father's school.

Servant no more, you became his *kei ma* 契媽,
contract mother, or godmother.
A gold chain for an umbilical cord,
my grandmother would say.
In family photos, you tried to stand in her place.
But where was the contract, the *kei* 契？ Lost

in a nursing home, a film of milk
over your eyes, you had nothing left to give.
Two slits down your earlobes waiting
for one word from a son's lips.

10,000 Thumbs

For Ma Wen Li
Zizhou County, China

The year's first rains found farmers
squatting outside the courthouse,
raindrops on open palms.

Loudspeakers announced five years
hard labor: the self-taught lawyer
spoke out against looting
in the name of taxes.

They all knew the camp,
though no one dared visit.
Every night they saw
his missing teeth
gleam in their rice.

In the fields, dust unsettled
with each strike of the hoe,
till the first hand curled to stamp
a thumbprint on papers
the well-schooled call a petition.

Ten thousand have followed,
thumbprints indelible
as the lines on their faces.

Whose hand will be the next to drop
a plough, a wrench, a rifle, handcuffs,
a needle, a pen, a poem
to bless this sheet of paper
the well-schooled call a petition,
the rest, a prayer?

40 Chicken Eggs

Zizhou County, China

carefully cradled,
though none would hatch,

stacked in a straw-lined basket,
an old man's only assets.

Each to be handed, shell intact,
to a passing palm for a few cents.

On the road to market, shouts
demanding taxes for rain and roads,

bridges closed, trucks,
uniforms, rifles,

fists, boots,
thud, crack.

40 eggs, shells intact,
on a motorbike, leaving

no witness in the crowd.

Early morning at the crossroads,
the old man slipped his neck in a noose,

throat dry as a river dammed upstream.

The Monk and the Rifle

During the monsoon, the monks vowed not to leave the monastery, for fear their footsteps might crush worms or larvae newly hatched in the rain: translucent, unfurling, some invisible to the naked eye. They vowed not to cut stems, not to cut leaves, not to cross rivers. They prayed for all sentient beings. Among them were two friends, Tenzin and Kalsang.

As the sky cleared, they prayed: if I have inadvertently killed anyone or anything, harmed anyone or anything, offended anyone or anything, I ask for forgiveness. Their vows lifted, they raised a large tent in celebration. Some were playing Sho, others bathing in the river when news of a protest arrived: monks from another monastery in Lhasa had been arrested. Tenzin and his friends feigned indifference, but whispered over the rolling dice.

They gathered before the monastery's protector, the horse-headed deity, Tadrin. Among them were Kalsang's cousin, Tashi, and Tenzin. Holding silk *katas* knotted into a circle, they vowed to stay together, suffer together, die together, and hold back from violence only. Kalsang was not ready; he had to take care of a teacher. He promised to stand by as witness, and if need be, take Tenzin to the hospital, body and tell his family.

Early morning, Kalsang drove Tenzin to Jokhang Temple in a tractor. They embraced and parted, two monks in lay clothing. Others in their group had arrived separately. On the crowded street, they pretended not to know one another until the first shout: "Free Tibet!" Tenzin began to run with thirty others around the Bakhor, shouting. The first round, a few pedestrians joined them; by the second, there were hundreds; by the third, they could no longer see the end of the crowd. As they ran, their voices grew, till they turned a corner to find a Chinese army truck blocking their path. The police sectioned off the first hundred and began to herd them away. Tenzin was one of them.

Soldiers started shooting at children who appeared on rooftops, cheering. Kalsang wrested a rifle from a sniper's hands. Instead of shooting, he raised it high above his head, and tried to smash it against the sidewalk; the rifle did not break. He was about to try again when a bullet from another rifle killed him.

Chopa tsewa mepa; Tawa tenjung.
Action - non-violent; View- dependent arising

A House of Paper

On a balcony, a girl lights a lantern.
Paper unpleats into a cylinder of light.
She sways her arm to anticipate the wind.
She knows happiness is a flame
rising straight in a house of paper.

In a house of paper, the walls
are lined with tales of the moon:
an empress once stole an elixir
from her husband. Some say
she was greedy; others, that she saved
the people from her tyrant husband,
his thirst for immortality.
She swallowed, and drifted
into the sky. She lives yet,
a demi-goddess, in exile on the moon.
By her side, a woodcutter
chops a self-healing tree;
a rabbit grinds herbs
with mortar and patient pestle.

While the night-blooming cereus unfolds,
the girl knows it is safe to light candles.
Tomorrow, when voices quarrel,
she will hide in a house of paper.

The girl asks for one more story.
Her mother tells her to look in the sky.
The moon is about to overflow into tomorrow.

Trade Winds

The Peabody Essex Museum, Salem, Massachusetts

A seamless ivory globe in a glass case: carved petals part
around an inner orb punctured with crosses precise
as logic. Under the crosses, another lobe bears
diamond-shaped piercings. Each layer shields
more of the next: concentric ivory spheres
carved around a hollow pith. Insert a
needle, a drop of opium at the tip.
At dead center, spheres resolve
into a whirlpool and spiral
down into an ocean
pacific.

Fore and Aft

        This tea I mete lifts me into the morning.
    Dried,
fermented,

        once hardened for journey, the leaves
     unfurl. I let them steep
without ritual.

        My mother's father poured hot water over
     his teaware
while the tea steeped.

        He knew when to stop, so the bitter
     came
clean.

        Sleep defying tea, leaves of the Chinese camellia,
     plucked from
fog,

        sold first for silver, then for somniferous mud,
     vengeance of Morpheus,
opium.

        Armed ships, deftly rigged fore and aft, sailed the seas
     and plied rivers.
Some bore

        the Union Jack, bold strokes like
     the ideogram for rice,
Others flew

        a banner spangled with stars, or flowers,
     or the fireworks
of war.

When the smoke cleared, guns remained, solid
     as a city on borrowed
time.

     Smoke and the convection of dreams clouded the story
          of an opium addict who gave away
a daughter,

          my father's mother, to his wife's childless friend.
     Once adopted,
she never answered

          her birth mother again, never forgave
     the choice to keep her sister,
the beauty.

          She spent her youth studying mirrors,
     mercurial thieves
of time.

          Quicksilver had come by sea from California,
     where Chinese miners inhaled
fumes of insanity.

          I drink the fragrance of tea in the hulls
     of armed clippers
long-sparred,

          low to water, lofty canvasses to *clip the speed*
     from the last inch
of wind,

          swift privateers, bearers of slaves,
     and other perishable
cargo.

*The Baltimore clipper type of sailing craft is a delicate creation
not unlike a fine violin or
a thoroughbred*

*racehorse with the ultimate purpose for its existence
being the only one thing—
performance.*

The first tea of the year to arrive in London
yielded
the highest.

The clipper *Nightingale* cut her first waves in New Hampshire
with her sharp bow
and sleek hull,

her figurehead, the soaring soprano, Jenny Lind. She raced tea
from Shanghai to London in a record
91 days.

For her next owner, she sailed to the coast
of Africa.
A sloop of war

found her at Kabenda with men, women, and children,
chained between decks,
and more

waiting on the beach. Fever took many
en route
to Liberia.

The ocean of oblivion hid their stench, and ferried
her Captain Bowen,
Prince of Slavers,

port to port, to carry on his secret trade
in small winds
and pleasant weather.

A shipwright built his wooden craft
on cradle
and cribwork,

carved the keel, her spine, the frame, her ribs,
from fine-grained
oak,

beams, deck and ceiling planks,
from dense, resinous
pine,

spars from Sitka spruce and Douglas fir,
trunnels from
locust,

curved braces from the sweeping limbs of live oak,
knees from the roots
of larch.

The vessel rigged, the shipwright knocked out
trigger timbers to ease her
into birth waters.

What did he know of the arms on board
to guard her
course and cargo?

Swivel guns, close-range, wide-arced,
to point at rebellion
on deck;

    iron carriage guns, cast in one piece,
   thick-breeched
for propulsion;

    blunderbusses, thunderguns of loud report,
   large bore,
wide-mouthed

    as captive jaws pried open with *speculum oris*,
   force feeding
to quell

    the quiet insurrection of hunger,
   wide-mouthed
as songs

    of lamentation to the strings of banjar,
   after dance coerced at point
of whiplash,

    dance of raw flesh against iron shackles
   in ankle-to-ankle
proximity,

    wide-mouthed as a pretty woman losing her teeth
   to Captain Philippe Liot's fist
as he forced her,

    before he clamped the mouth of a 10 year-old,
   and pried her
open beneath him.

    Sold, price reduced, in Saint Domingue,
   the woman died
in two weeks.

        I drink beads of sweat on cane field slaves,
    tears
of the skin.

        I drink gold paint on the spiral stairs
    of Bristol
mansions.

        I drink molasses distilled to pure escape
    in the shackles
of addiction.

        I drink cocoa and coffee, brown ivory
    on the backs
of sold children.

        I drink the cold winds of hunger. I drink
    the mirage of blue glass beads
in a growing desert.

        I drink raindrops of knowledge reviving desert fish
    dormant
in mud.

        I drink the clean air of restraint. I drink my fill
    from a clear
glass.

        I drink truth, lucent from ice to vapor. I drink
    the cooling of war
and desire.

        I drink to my children, not far
    from the wrecked
  ship

            in tide pools star-spangled
        with possibilities.
I drink

            the metallic memory of tea,
        I drink its torpid
history.

The Tint of Dawn

A metal sheath the tint of dawn
shines untarnished on black onyx.
I leave the bracelet unhinged
on a satin cushion—gold,
wisdom of an illiterate servant
who called my father son.
In times of war, banknotes
were bundled and weighed
while gold held its luster.

From my grandparents' garden,
my mother's sister dug up gold bars
she surrendered to the proletariat.
Uniform, countable, molded for exchange,
the bars bore straight lines and angles,
not the manifolds and curves
of Atahualpa's ransom:
ewers, salvers, ears of corn,
fountain with bathing animals,
altars—the sun's radiance recast
into coins mercenaries tendered
for silk and spices, and sunk
into the underground hoards
of Chinese merchants.

I dissolve gold in *aqua regia*
to hide it in plain sight of an invading army;
I stretch it into thread, not for embroidery,
but to transmit secret impulses;
I trade gold for salt, ounce for ounce,
dumb barter between landlocked miners
and traders past the range of camels.

In the watershed of sweat
between the Vaal and the Olifants,
I make masks of black miners
from gold hammered translucent.
I forge their signatures in Purple of Cassius
in the smallest hours between light and darkness.

A Day in British Hong Kong

June, 1989

6 a.m.	The papers are sold out. News from Beijing, my daily cocaine.
6:30 a.m.	In the bathroom mirror, I see the untrampled face of a student; my school badge, three neat letters on a metal plate, firm on my chest.
7:30 a.m.	A few black ribbons are safety-pinned to chalk blue uniforms. On my best friend's copy of Ming Pao, the shock of red on b&w newsprint: mangled bicycles, anonymous faces on concrete.
8:00 a.m.	Ourfatherinheavenholybeyournameyour kingdomcomeyourwillbedone… Our homeroom teacher declares the bulletin board has no space for politics. Government policy is the full stop of all sentences.
10:20 a.m	In my whey-colored exercise book, the sum of vectors is the swirl of my thumbprint, newspaper inked. How to combine magnitude and direction when the cycling blades of ceiling fans overhead are the only constants? How to measure the vectors of flight from Tiananmen Square, the sudden arrest of death?
12:00 p.m.	Lunch. We fill the mouths of envelopes with photocopied news, address them to schools, factories, anywhere in mainland China, and feed them through slots on silent, crimson pillars. Queen Elizabeth's lips are sealed with a smile on every stamp.
2:20 p.m.	Economics and Public Affairs. Our teacher reminds us not to wear our uniforms to rallies. We will not be caroling at the Peninsula Hotel, pinning corsages on diners' lapels.
4:00 p.m.	We spill like vomit into the streets, hurling slogans at Li Peng, Deng Xiao Ping—a conversation with the skies above.

6:00 p.m.   The avenues are clogged with school uniforms, white rolled-up sleeves, shirts soiled with motor oil, shoes synchronized to test the natural frequency of tyranny, the rhythm it takes to amplify waves till a structure crumbles. An unfinished experiment.

9:00 p.m.   In the quiet after slogans and songs, we hold candles, and find, in the darkness that follows, the after-image of candlelight, how an idea can consume the body, and remain.

Summer at Judgment

Hong Kong, 1993

On a dance floor packed spandex tight,
synthesizers hypnotize our heartbeat.
Each step a further forgetting,
each beat a blank square in a crossword
of friends, relatives, countries and dates.

In the countdown to '97, we've
parceled ourselves overseas,
returning summers only. Lips
to the rims of tepid cocktails,
we ask no questions after childhood
friends long traded away as used stamps.

We breathe not a word of the clubowner's
father, his gang-spun roulette monopoly.
Strobes sample us into polaroids.
Every other instant is darkness.

Between trips to the cinema, I lift
the receiver to news of a gang fight
at Judgment. A wayward blow blinded
one of us, émigré home vacationing.

Unreeling kicks by an action hero,
I splice a new film from frames denied
by the blink of my eyes: myself an extra
dancing to the beat of choreographed
killing, a nightclub entrance stamp
not yet faded from the back of my hand.

All That She Wants

is another baby.
She's gone tomorrow,
but all that she wants...

A pop tune slips between the metallic
pant legs of machine gun techno.
Tourists of the night, eyes open
only for the occasional backward
glance. There is one night spinning
between London, New York,
Buenos Aires and Hong Kong:
one fashion, one perfume,
one fantasy of letting go.

It's not easy to live in the moment
when the moment loops back
like a pirated pop tune:

All That She Wants
comes back as *Weeping Mary*
in Cantonese.

What survives jet lag and translation
is desire packaged and sold: a waft
of cigarette smoke lifting like a question
from an upturned palm, from the collar
of a black leather jacket in a nightclub,
a church, collegiate gothic, where mirrors
sell immaculate sex without conception.
There are no statues, only dancers
wearing the crucifix like a charm
swaying over a womb forgotten.

Landing

Since landing, I have greeted more strangers
than Hello Kitty and *maneki neko* combined.
I am careful to heed the people-mover's advice:
Ashimoto ni gochūi kudasai 足元にご注意ください.
Please watch your step.
The false bottom of a *bento* hastily purchased
before catching a train is every traveler's warning.
The glide of the *shinkansen* is facile, almost
frictionless. I can't tell how fast we are going. I fall,
motionless as a stone, one of thousands in a rock garden
of stationary waves. A tour guide calls to his flock
in a language impervious to me. I find myself in
Ryoanji, and set off again. I would be a petal flitting
in the wind, but for the my grandmother's story:

She is standing beside a bed, young and unmarried
in wartime Hong Kong. A friend poses
a question from under his blanket:
Would you rather give it to me, or to the Japanese soldiers?
Soldiers are hunting door to door for single women.
She climbs in. Five children and eight grandchildren
have branched from the bed, and regret heavy
as a blanket pawned and redeemed.

One quarter of a lost gamble, I have come to learn
the language my grandmother escaped.
The voice of my Japanese teacher follows me:
Hiroshima ni itte kudasai 広島に行って下さい.
Instead, I wander through the temples of Kyoto
and rest in the home of strangers. At dinner, my host
darts from the strength of the yen to the registry of language
in the brain, and pauses abruptly for a deep bow, back straight,
palms on the table: *sumimasen* すみません, an apology for the war.

How to learn the art of prostration? Start slowly.
Kiss the ground with knees, shins, thighs, belly, chest, palms and ears.
Listen for the first fallen hair of Hiroshima.

The Seal

A Japanese officer in occupied China held a military seal with the power to move rations. He was scrupulous in his accounting. One day, unable to reconcile quantities of rice, he began to suspect someone else had been using his seal.

The alleys of logic led him to a Chinese man subordinate, a poor man who took care of horses. He questioned the man, who fell to his knees. In the accounting terms of the day, a spoonful of rice was worth more than a Chinese life. The officer, despite his uniform, quietly spared his subordinate.

The two men met again in the heat and blood lust of August, after the surrender. A Japanese life was less than worthless, a collaborator's liability. The Chinese man sheltered his benefactor, family and all, and stowed them away on a homebound ship under the wide blanket of night.

The Boots and the Weary Bird

for Inukai Tsuyoshi 犬養毅, last civilian prime minister of pre-war Japan, poet, and friend of Sun Yat-sen 孫中山

The gate to my house is a gap in the brushwood hedge
allowing the fresh breeze to flow in with ease.

When the assassins arrived,
Inukai stayed to greet them.

...inside is a heavenly grotto,
free from the dross of mundane affairs...

The first trigger summoned an empty cartridge.
"You can shoot anytime. Let's sit down and talk."

A white belt of mist girdles the mountains at morning;
at evening, the peaks turn crimson in a sunset glow.

He folded his arms at his chest in a gentle self-embrace
and led the uniformed intruders to a sitting room.

Now and again an ocean of clouds surges down,
swiftly casting a shroud of dim drizzle over the view.

"Do you have to keep your boots on? How about taking them off?"
He took a cigarette from its box and motioned the officers to join him.

Painting and poetry— so venerated since antiquity;
yet can they compare with the wonders of nature?

They fired several bullets into his head. He asked the maid
to light the blood-soaked cigarette between his fingers.

All over the mountains, autumn leaves blaze yellow and red;

an icy stream cuts a band of blue ribbons in its downward flow.

"The young people who were here a minute ago—
tell them to come back. I want to talk with them."

Returning to the nest, weary birds sing out for joy.
Ragged clouds drift over the peaks, then vanish without a trace.

He asked for them three times,
then curled on his side, as if awaiting birth.

Cartographies

Cartographies

                i.

Encase a globe in a cylinder,
illuminate from within, watch
continents cast shadows

on a curved wall: intimate
where the wall is tangent,
the rest, variously distorted.

                ii.

 datum: a touch
              of sunlight
on the back   of my   hand

                iii.

Though the imperial scale of a map
offers direct proportion, the length
of this coastline will grow
if I measure every volute:
inbite, rock, grain of sand...

Tell me, roughly, how far apart we are.
We will find each other on faint trails.

                iv.

White crowned sparrows
cry *wit wit* as I draw near.
I would have mistaken
their alarm for song
had I not eavesdropped earlier.

I search for a scale
to notate their whistle.

    v.

Feather boa kelp, bull whip kelp,
green pin cushion, surf grass, sea lettuce,
Turkish towel, sea palm, and scouring pad algae
know nothing of the names we give them.

Some drift. Others vie for rock
as nations dispute islands in open sea:

 Senkaku/ Tiao Yu Tai
  Nansha/ Spratlys / Truong Sa / Kalayaan

    vi.

I watch a woman write calligraphy
on the floor of a Luoyang square:
strokes evaporate within steps.
What's left is breath.

    vii.

Metacarpals, metatarsals,
femur, tibia, fibula, anvil—
bones nominally distinct;
joints, fulcrums of logic.

Surgeons run scalpels
along specified striae:
sartorius, soleus,
latissimus dorsi…

Lovers do not delineate
the smooth gradient

from neck to shoulder,
heel to ankle, waist to thigh.

viii.

Flatten an orange peel with care:
insert slits at regular intervals;
carve an icosahedron, perhaps;
tear, unfold, compress.

Show the flattened peel to someone
who has never seen an orange.

What lies in the stolen dimension?

ix.

    Earth   throws its bulge
  outward,   spinning.

While   words coalesce,
   Earth fissures,
           liquefies,
     slides
into itself.

What is your name, again?

x.

Don't stop here—
  blue startle,
this photo graph
  of Earth,
      skin,
    flesh,
  ingress.

Half a Duet

the day we eloped   the sun was exacting

each grain of sand pellucid as water
           the horizon *forever*   lucid

I read you a poem I wrote

if for a moment, I should forget….

忘不了   忘不了

I can't forget   I can't forget

but I've forgotten the poem I read to you

in the place of refuge   *Pu'uhonua O Hōnaunau*
            the day we eloped

          we knew little of
    of sanctuaries
Pu'uhonua   a sanctuary from death sentences

     if you made your way there
           you would be safe

              we were tourists
         in the word *forever*
   we knew little
of defeated warriors then
        of war
  of
kapu   taboo
       of kapu breakers

                    of forgiveness
               of the word *forever*

                         if
                    for a moment
                       I should forget....
忘不了　忘不了
忘不了你的錯　忘不了你的好

I can't forget　I can't forget
I can't forget your mistakes   *I can't forget*
                                                  the good in you

     you pushed me   the gift of time,
three times   the rent you paid
        then came
            your denial   freedom
              as if you could
                force open   silence like
     the camera of my mind   silver halide
                     expose the
negatives
          and dribble paint over them

if
for a moment
I should forget....
            忘不了　忘不了
      忘不了你的錯　忘不了你的好
          忘不了雨中的散步
I can't forget our walks in the rain
    we hiked through open valleys carved by glaciers
with only the wind and a soft drizzle between us

you showed me the foundation of a farmhouse

long abandoned flooded and drained
masonry returning to stone overgrown
with everything I can't remember

忘不了　忘不了
忘不了你的錯　忘不了你的好
忘不了雨中的散步
也忘不了那風裏的擁抱
I can't forget our embraces in the wind
I can't remember the Manhattan avenue
where you first held my hand

I arched my back
when you whispered in my ear
the sound of wind into wind
against the rush of passing cars

I can't forget
your grip　firm but tender
like the first step from a blustery street
into a heated room

I can't name the pitch
of glass to glass
when you said over dinner
here's to a future together
I think you said
here's to a future together
忘不了　忘不了
忘不了你的錯　忘不了你的好
忘不了雨中的散步　也忘不了那風裏的擁抱

忘不了　忘不了
忘不了你的淚　　　　　　　　忘不了你的笑

I can't forget your tears
   after your mother's death
     you smashed a stool
    against the wall
   at a pause in our conversation
at her funeral
you cried for a moment
  on the shoulder of a woman
your mother liked
       and you once loved
     whose hair was the same color
       as your sister's

I can't forget your laughter
  we played catch like kids
  in your shoebox
  of an apartment
  I laughed when
  you caught me
  you would always catch me

忘不了　忘不了
忘不了你的錯　忘不了你的好
忘不了雨中的散步　也忘不了那風裏的擁抱

忘不了　忘不了
忘不了你的淚　忘不了你的笑
忘不了葉落的惆悵　也忘不了那花開的煩惱

I can't forget the melancholy
of falling leaves

I can't forget the vexing
flowers

you lay between sheets of silence
   in pallid wintry sun
     ginkos on the avenue
leafbare
   silence like sheetrock
    I asked you again
if you wanted children
 you answered, for once: *I don't know*

              the risks we took

              skin to skin

if you tell me again:
I'll never love anyone the way I loved you

I'll answer with a *fermata*

I'll answer again: we were tourists in the word *forever*
in Mexico City the air was the temperature of our bodies
the ceiling fan spun high above us
I was on my back, dizzy
our bodies were never so soft
I raised my knees as you entered me
I knew I would conceive

I'll answer again:

I can still play my half of Saint-Saëns' The Swan
I can still play my half of Ave Maria, Schubert's and Gounod's
I can still play my half of Jesus Joy of Man's Desiring
I can still attempt my half of our Rachmaninoff Sonata
I can't remember the name of the Debussy we played

reaching, reaching

I can't erase the music we played

I can't erase my words to our toddler:
Santa Claus does not exist

I can't erase your words:
you don't know what you're saying
you don't know what this means to me
you don't know what this means to my family

one push for each sentence

I can't erase your denial:
I didn't push you; I put my hand on your shoulder

as if you could
force open the camera of my mind
expose the negatives

and dribble paint over them

if you tell me again
I'll never love anyone the way I loved you

I can only translate this song for you
   a song I can remember
   a song I can forget

忘不了　忘不了
忘不了你的錯　忘不了你的好
忘不了雨中的散步　也忘不了那風裏的擁抱

忘不了　忘不了
忘不了你的淚　忘不了你的笑
忘不了葉落的惆悵　也忘不了那花開的煩惱

寂寞的長巷　而今斜月清照
冷落的鞦韆　而今迎風輕搖
它重復你的叮嚀　一聲聲　忘了　忘了
它低訴我的衷曲　一聲聲　難了　難了

a desolate alley flushed with moonlight
a lone swing swaying in the wind
repeating your reprimands, voices forgotten
whispering my heart's song, endless, endless

Portrait of Winds

i.

How much of yourself do you see in me
as you lean back from a kiss?
Come close again, closer
than the focal point of your eyes.
I. Not I.
Kiss me. Break the mirror between us.

ii.

Which currents shall I ride towards you?
Hand me a moving map:
water feathers from the equator,
whorls along coastlines.
I will reckon.
I will drift.
I will propel myself.
I will swirl in Coriolis blossoms.

iii.

My breath glances off your ear
and returns to caress the space above my lips.
I could draw you with my eyes closed:
a portrait of winds.

iv.

Excavate. Lay bare
the strata of my history:
the reversal of poles long ago
written in layers of rock,
the slow drift of plates
once solid as pledges of love.

I have as many names as past lovers,
exotic terrane left by collision.
You will find their names written beneath my skin.

    v.

$h = a/d$,

where d is distance,

a, the apparent height of objects,

h, the true height.

When he kissed me daily, I knew him by the bend in his neck.
His silhouette is now the size of my palm.
The distance between us is the ratio: *then* to *now*.

I knew his apparition only.
If I had gauged the distance between us,
I would have known who he was.

    vi.

You show me a piece of broken porcelain.
I pick it up and break it, again, in half.
I did not mean to test its strength.
This haste, this urge to know,
this sudden learning of a brittle truth.

    vii.

I circle my arms around your neck;
you place your hands on my waist.
You reach for my hand; I listen.
You fall silent; I wait.
The touching of lips in greeting and farewell.
Sunrise. Sunset.

I mark this day in a journal of rituals.

        viii.

No single map can mark
this expanse from me to you.
I can only offer an atlas of charts,
each a modest moment:
this evening I listen to the ring
of your finger on bisque porcelain;
I note the tessellation of cracks
on the earthen surface of your statues.
Above us, the moon continues beyond metaphor.

        ix.

If there are manifolds unseen,
we must ask each other:

Where are you hiding?

        x.

If I am moving towards you at constant speed,
and you are at rest, one could also say:
you are moving towards me, and I am at rest.

        xi.

A migratory bird needs no maps.
There is a compass within.
There is memory.
There is ritual.
There is camaraderie.
There is the self-symmetry of feathers
in the trained freedom of wings.

What storms have risen from this flight?
Between destinations,
wings stir a country of winds.

        xii.

Mountain is slow wave;
wave, quickened mountain.

Travel through me.

Where Indigo Meets Azure

Show me where indigo meets azure
and I will draw a line in the ocean
with my finger. I will take you
to a girl named *Aabi* for blue,
for her grandmother *Aiko* 愛子,
for *ai* 愛: indigo, love.
I will write *ai* 愛 in desert sand,
where merchants once spilled cobalt
in sandstorms, where blue returned
on porcelain, guarded by swords.
Show me war in the desert,
and I will intercept pigeons
to read you love letters written in ink.
At the end of the desert, we will watch
a raven on a tree limb turn into a dove
with an olive branch in his beak.

Show me blue from beyond the sea,
and I will take you to a boy
named *Lazuli* for the stone of azure.
But here we must leave behind
the pigment once worth its weight in gold,
adorning the holy and the royal, forget
aphrodisiacs and superstitions of old,
sit down and break bread
with a boy who eats no meat,
drinks no milk or honey. Do not ask
the name of his country. He lives above
the bending of light, where water
and air are transparent as love.

Wishbone

I learn my body bone by bone.
My fingers articulate the journey
as on the named keys of a piano:
I begin with the clavicles, twin keys
to unlock my chest, a finger's space
between them; wishbone unfused,
an invitation, a wish open as the path
between breasts unknown to suckle.
Around my heart's impetus are ribs,
floating and firm. The lift and fall,
lift and fall of the cage hinges
on the honest labor of lungs.
My fingers dance on my animal belly.
The baring of its flesh is trust
on its way to the final shock of fur.
In a lover, I seek the desire to feel
fine bones and leave them intact.

Flotsam

i.

Succulent ribbons on wet sand.
Long tubes with bulbous ends.
You open a broken vessel
to show me its nourishing sap:
a fertile beginning.

You turn towards me. I place
my palm on your face,
and spread my fingers to receive
what has come our way.

ii.

On a rocky beach, sea stars
by the hundreds, spent, discolored
refugees from a distant storm.
I do not ask where.
There are underwater storms
beyond the cartographer's hand,
like the last hidden battle
in your mother's body.
We can do nothing but stand.
Scavenging gulls circle overhead.

Waves rasp against rocks:
sand to shale, shale to sand.

iii.

Snow engulfs your mother's house
in the first days of her absence.
The ones to break the stillness

are not the gulls she favored,
but two doves, bold and guileless.
They wait at the feeder.
We stop short of naming them.

      iv.

We find a makeshift shelter
of driftwood, and play house.
A sandbank shields us from the wind.
Two grown children, we play.
Our house is open to the tender
fingers of the rain. There is wet
growing in a place beyond where.

Common Flower

For Dorothy

You try to teach me the flowering
order of your garden in spring:
snowdrops, hyacinths, daffodils, tulips...
no, hyacinths, tulips, daffodils, snowdrops...
A forgotten rosary.
You would have me send down
your grandson's roots
in newly thawed Northeastern soil.

In the silence between us, a common flower
grows, a red hibiscus leeward from your house,
a transplant: flower of Caribbean winds
bearing word of your half-sisters,
flower of my childhood strolls
in the mushroomed woods of Asia.
Flower of blood. Nomadic, animal flower.

I note the growing caesuras
between your breaths, your paling skin.

In the silence after you, your grandson and I
will make love in yet another country.
We will see a man feed hibiscus
to an iguana among Mayan ruins.
Scarlet, vegetable flower.

Our daughter will come to us
on the wild tongues of the Pacific,
the coast of your birth.

In a world where flowers travel,
it is impossible to be strangers.

Brooding

My daughter is learning to draw eggs
as one would hold them, to gentle
the perfect circle of a sea turtle egg,
the ellipse of a beetle's egg,
the fanciful tendrils of a dogfish egg case,
the sizable, solid ostrich oval.
Will she learn to brood?
When will she learn it is far easier
to crack an egg than hatch one?

Letter from Sister to Brother

Play me the song of Earth from outer space.
The camera you shot into the sky
orbits in silence, a dime-sized device
on a satellite. Though I long to spy
on glacial rivers and estuaries
emptying into the seas like dendrites,
what I seek, beyond the geography
of Earth approximated in digits,
is your coronary map, with jet streams,
doldrums, trades, westerlies and hurricanes.
Hear the tenuous whistle of the wind?
Your heart's calling to its sibling, the brain
orbiting in space, the vacuum between
them, a sparse childhood almost forgotten.

To Unborn Sons

What languages have you heard
straining through your mothers' tongues
into your surrounding waters?

Mine is a vocabulary of greetings,
souvenirs from times of mock peace:

guten tag　　*zo sun* 早晨　　*namaste*
mata ashita また明日　　*hasta mañana*
shalom　　*salaam*

Teach me how to say *sorry* in Arabic,
Pashto and Farsi, and I will teach
the son astir in my belly.

In your negative age, counting to zero,
speak to one another in the language
of the unborn, the language of water.
Tomorrow, a different light will fall.

Who among you will befriend another
in a land not your own?

Who among you will negotiate
in a currency not your own?

Who among you will ask for mercy
in a language not your own?

Who among you will live to tell?
Which language will you choose?

Will you recall the pause
in your pregnant mother's pulse,
a woman's premonition,
before composing herself to carry on?

Aspiration

A lubricous   blood-drenched
push.   Life   delivers itself.
Cord   severed,   the afterbirth,
like offal,
      plumps
      down
            on a metal dish.

Afterbirth, the color of earth.

The   first   aspiration
of a newborn   is breath.
Mother and child   exhale.
Staggered
         relief.
The mother sleeps,   yielding
like   her   newborn's skin.

Panhandlers   appear in the emulsion
of her   dreams, supplicant strangers:

We   were once babies   too.
Where   does your love   end?

Open Circles

"...the U.S. military launched yesterday Operation Ivy Serpent"

I dream   a lizard sliding into water
                             streamlines into a fish
     dream   I am a woman without
                             a snake within

spine upright
        I walk among bipeds
   speak their language
                till rumors of a snake
                      lisp across the room
                                   I slither
      through an open window
         wend my way in grass

            I wake in a country dropping
   metaphors in war

I seek
     the company of serpents
                    beyond paradise lost or redeemed
     Rainbow Serpent   Quetzalcoatl
     sentinels of water
     Nü Kua   half-woman   half-snake
   who kneaded us from clay
         Cecrops   snake-tailed founder of Athens
  the healing serpent
      on the staff of Asclepius
               open circles
      the weaving of myths about a hidden axis
         the broad sweep of an integral

     two supple curves like an equal sign spell *almost*

like the mark of a question   the dance
                              of a mordent on a musical note
                    the suture of open wounds
with sibilant threads of song

California Rain Song

Rain is tinning the roof of the old chicken coop
        where doe and fawn shelter.
            They forage

under the wild plum tree that grew back from root stock
        after a lawn-mower topped
            the apricot graft.

Rain questions neither graft nor stock
        in its glissando down the trunk of the fig,
            first crop of the Fertile Crescent,

coaxes California poppies, free of sleep's swollen satchel,
        twangs lemon leaves, and drops
            a soft percussion on the rind of its fruit.

Though rain has swept through the mountains of Asia,
        it cannot recall the provenance
            of citrus astringent, sweet or bitter;

it does not ask if the spines
        of the prickly pear are redundant
            outside the desert.

There is no discussion in rain's polyphony;
        it nourishes what is here,
            the cultivated and the wild:

calla lily, oxalis, clover, bluegrass, sage bush,
        fescue, fennel, rosemary, black bamboo, blackberries,
            manzanita, juniper, avocado, persimmon, kiwi...

What does rain dissolve from the air that seeps into root and leaf?
        What transpires again from leaf to air?
            What gravitates?

In sodden clay, water collects and percolates
                past gopher skeletons, reptilian slough,
                          shards of glass, plastic pots,

and the mouth of a buried well—a corona of stones.
                What leaches from the past
                          into the current underground?

I must ask, though rain will not tell me
                the story behind the snapshot
                          my husband found in our living room:

a teenage boy with glasses, braces and an awkward smile.
                The elderly woman who sold us the house
                          returned, and took the photo back in silence.

I can only guess the subterranean path of rain
                by signs of unsettling earth:
                          buckled concrete, tilted walls.

Streams seen and unseen run downhill, perpendicular
                to the old cow path from ranch
                          to slaughterhouse.

Did the same streams run through these hills when the first cowhands
                slaughtered cattle, kept the hides for leather
                          and exposed the flesh to grizzlies?

Cattle gathered by creeks for shade and water,
                trampled the streambed contours,
                          left fish in riffles with no shelter.

Where grasses and wildflowers once paved the hillside,
                eucalyptus now grows. An investor scattered
                          millions of seeds.

                .

New-growth eucalyptus would *chip when planed*
                and crack when dried,
                              its leaves form crowns of fire.

I leaf through time, where words patter; drops collect into rivulets
                from colophon to gutter. There are rivers older
                              than the mountains rising in their path.

Where a creek slowed into estuary above high tide,
        water heaped alluvial on a mound
                      overgrown with brambles.

Men carved into its eastern side,
        dissected the cone's curved face
                      with straight railroad lines.

The train whistle had the pitch of keening, timbre hollow
        as the human bones in the mound,
                porous as the bones of shorebirds above.

Rain quavered through silt, gravel, and two millennia of bones:
            gopher, raccoon, wild cat, deer, elk, wolf, grizzly bear,
                      cormorant, turtle, skates, thornback....

No 6. Grave of a child a little over a year old
                found in the tunnel in stratum VIIa
                        at a depth of 17 feet below the surface.

It lay from north to south upon a bed of charcoal and red earth....
        A number of shell beads...lay in rows from the neck down
                along the body and were originally necklaces....

Men came again, truncated the mound, and raised a pavilion
        to waltz on bones. The creek trilled on as couples danced
                on skeleton pairs buried thigh to thigh,

and mothers whose fetuses had never seen light.
        Rain alone could not wash away these bones.
                The maw of a steam shovel swallowed the mound.

A paint factory rose, stained mud red beyond cleansing,
               redder than ochre sprinklings
                             on bones rubbery with arsenic and lead.

What can rain dissolve? Silence is the rustle of shopping bags.
               Spoonbills sleep, beaks buried in wings.
                             Metal cranes rest across the inlet.

Where the tide leaves salt crystals on grass, a red-tailed hawk circles.
               A chant evaporates into the air,
                           recollecting scattered bones.

Paper Rain

At the World Financial Center, a gaggle
of fresh graduates lunch at a long table.
A view of the Hudson invites the eye
to own it all: barges, slow-moving
beasts of burden, passenger ants
on ferries, toy-sized sailboats and buoys.
At the head of the table, a middle-aged man
intones: *Make no mistake. This is Rome.*

A young woman turns to a modern painting
on the wall: two ink blots, uneven in size.
Curious spectacles, lopsided eyes, inkblots
insisting on asymmetry. She looks away
before her eyes obey their prescription.

At rush hour, she makes her way through
the Winter Garden, where palm trees aspire
to a glass ceiling. Past rotating doors,
down a shadowy subway stairwell,
a grown man weeps, head in hands,
the stench of urine sharp as a hypodermic
needle. On the platform, a steel drum rolls
like spilled cherries. She tries to remember
why she is here, which train will take her home.
A train so confident it smears expletives
on tunnel walls. Where it emerges,
cardboard huts huddle over steam vents.

A friend calls to say: *It's raining
singed paper on the Brooklyn Bridge.*

Quotidian

My newborn coos as I wipe milk
from the folds of his neck.
My husband slides his hammer
into his back pocket
and climbs down the ladder.
I trace the flight path
of a hummingbird into bottlebrush.
Dusk settles like dust after rain.
My son is quiet, but I am restless.

It is dawn in Fallujah:
a soldier lifts a child's blanket
with the mouth of his machine gun;
a doctor peers out the window,
afraid to leave home;
an elderly woman holds
her daughter's limp hand
and lies to her about the stillborn;
two men drag a stranger
from the line of fire, his hair a brush
painting blood on the sidewalk.
The day has just begun.

On my street, a car stops
to let doe and fawn cross.
My husband spills a glass of water.
Libation, perhaps, but enough
to atone for the evening's serenity?

The GI Bill

Before you put your life on the recruiting
table next to Payless Shoes, look across
the street at Colonel Sanders and the Visa logo—
Eat Now, Pay Later. Before setting your hopes
on the starched white collar of a professor
and the somber weight of books,
try this exercise in philosophy:
You are either with us or against us.
Is this a tautology? Ponder
this lesson in physics: at a checkpoint,
a warning shot bounces off the ground
to kill a passenger of a van.
Was he with us, or against us?
A casual statistic. The central question,
of course, is one of semiotics:
WMD
Find the elusive signified, GI.
Before you put yourself on the line
between the signifier and the signified,
consider the loose wire by the roadside.

The Taste of Each

                    i.

The peel of quartered oranges made the edge of my mouth sting.
There were citrus cousins more appealing—
gum 甘 with peel like the loose-hanging skin of bulldogs,
They arrived in anonymous crates with the rousing winter air.
They were small ones, *gut* 桔, came in pots for Chinese New Year,
shining like gold.
We didn't ask their names or home countries: *calamansi, calamondin*.
The word *orange* was as familiar as *tsang* 橙.
Sunkist stickers were passport stamps for oranges
from the Sun, California to Hong Kong.

The earliest oranges burst forth on the Himalayan massif.
The first to appear in British Isles, brought by Spanish ships,
were bitter to the palate—the sweet came centuries later,
by seed, trade, and graft, through the Mediterranean,
where they basked, royal guests in conservatories of glass.

Words also branch:
nuranga, narang, naranj, naranja, arancia, orenge....
The taste of each lingers on the tongue.
The Persian *narang* refers not to the color,
but to the bitterness of the peel.

Apfelsine, sinaasappel: Chinese apples,
the German and the Dutch called them.

Oranges gave their name to the color *geoluhread,* yellow-red.
Marmalade's name grew from its own tree, next to honey and quince:
mel, melimelon, marmelo, marmalada....
A candymaker in Dundee shipped her chip marmalade,
peel preserved, to Sydney and Shanghai.
How much sweetness do we need to swallow the bitter?

Monterey Market in Berkeley sells blood oranges, kumquats,
Valencia oranges, tangelos, Seville oranges, Satsuma mandarins,
bergamot oranges, cara cara navel oranges, pommelos, pixie tangerines....

I am not nostalgic for a time and place
when oranges were exotic.
I relish their abundance.

ii.

Banana: the word has traveled far
from Wolof, Malinke, and Vai.
I have tasted bananas few hands have touched,
ripe when gravid under supple, brown peel.
Dai tsiu 大蕉: this fruit cannot cross oceans--
its journey is brief, from tree to soil.
I can't name aromas lost
in cultivars of spotless yellow,
thick skin over tapered bodies.

Banana: noun, currency, commodity.
United Fruit, Chiquita: proper nouns as fiction.
Bashō 芭蕉:

> *A banana plant in autumn winds –*
> *I listen to the drops of rain*
> *Fall into a basin at night.*

iii.

No one taught me how to eat fresh dates,
pale as wax, firm on a leafless branch.
My mouth puckered at the first taste.
I waited till they were soft, translucent,
wrinkled as fingers soaked in water;
I let the light sweetness rest on my tongue.

Halawi, medjool, dayri, zahidi, deglet noor....
I have tried to remember the taste of each,
but my tongue has failed me.
Under each name, I reserve a space
the size of a date for what I have yet to learn,
a place with no flavor, neither better nor worse
than what I think I already know.

The Reader

    i.

A house gecko
hangs upside down
on the fluorescent
bulb of my desk lamp:
under lucid flesh,
breathing heart,
the stay of the spine,
amazing intestines.
By lamplight, I
the unflinching gecko.

    ii.

In the crook of a trail,
a blue heron stands,
one ligneous foot in the stream.
A quicksilver fish
slides down his throat.
The plume on his head quivers.
The stream mends itself.
His foot, again, as root.

Sated, I cross the bridge.

    iii.

I walk toward the low of fog horns
and the swivel of light house beams:

    ...warn you...
        ...come to me...
   ...warn you...

iv.

A snail's underside ripples
up the glass door
to rooftop scents rarefied
beyond my ken.

v.

Under marjoram brush,
sudden mushrooms
rise above wood chips,
flags for detritus unseen.

vi.

Tomatoes on untrained vines
dwell close to warm ground,
swollen with the sun's musk.

vii.

In morning mist,
dew-drenched cobwebs
between car window and side mirror.

I too have built in the comfort of corners,
and what appears stationary.

viii.

Frogs on summer leaves.

My dear friend, who passed last summer,
taught me:

frog   *kaeru* 蛙
 return   *kaeru* 帰る

Tell me how to read frogs on summer leaves.

The Tale

I once lived in a landlocked town in a house on the edge
of the woods, near a stagnant pond or two, grass up to my waist.

I would thirst for rain, oceans distilled; I would stand in the squall,
and let rain blow in gusts like waves on my face, let raindrops

trickle down my neck till I burst, skin wrinkled,
cotyledon sprouting; I soaked in the rain like a wick;

I dreamed of waves murderous, amniotic, disgorging
aquatic fetuses, ingesting children

of the land; I wandered in search of water, the femur
of an ambulocetus to guide me.

Though rain courses through my hair, into my ears,
like a lover's fingers, I am no vessel for the rain.

I am fluent: the river in my father's name,
the flood in my mother's.

I pour myself into the river, into
the ocean I have crossed many times, each journey, a life.

My lives cross over, paths recombinant. I swim in any skin:
the selkie's pinniped pelt, the weaver maiden's skein;

I will not be stolen by lovers. I walk by day and swim by night.
I do not trade my voice

for the privilege of walking on land. Listen,
hear me sing: *Once, once, once upon a wave....*

More than a lover, I'm a chambered nautilus
from deep to shallow, shallow to deep.

I swim in waters of plasma, waters of dancing cilia,
ionic waters.

I swim through the pores of sponges, through the baleen
of whales. From the viscera of transparent fish,

I see vents teeming with edible sulphur--I read what earth
divulges. I ride the deep sea conveyor of salt.

Under glaciers and ice floes, salt flows unfrozen, a low cycle,
a thousand years, a moving museum.

I harvest from the incessant salt mill of the sea: memory--
an orange jacket my friend remembers,

but nothing of a boat drifting for days without water.
Treasure jettisoned, unmarked in low tide.

I swim to escape memories,
like a child who doesn't believe

rays of the sun can sear her flesh;
like a brush on a snare drum,

like airy echoes in the empty palace
of a conch,

to escape my lover, who mistook the ocean before him
for a tract of land bounded by language

and treaties inscribed by war.
I am rock turned into woman.

I am a woman who swims like water.
I swim towards guyots of friendship,

constants in the constant drift. I feed rich
upwelling with no intention but the warmth in my body,

light with nothing to light upon,
love intransitive. I hide

my many selves in a shoal.
I seem to swim within reach of the man I once loved.

He is blinded by the glint of ten thousand fins,
and sets fire to the surface of the sea.

I hold my breath and dive under.
There are gills on my jaws. I have almost forgotten

my tears do not alter the ocean.
There is salt enough. Listen,

listen to the ocean's lilting lullaby:
stray this-a-way, sway, sway….

I return to land and bear the pain
of splitting my tail in two:

I birth myself at the mouth of a cenote,
among the roots of mangroves

among blind
fish who do not see me,

though they taste the bleeding
between my legs;

they live in a maze of tunnels:
some dead ends, others entrances to the sea.

I rise towards land--by land, I mean what is covered by air,
not water. I pluck mangrove leaves

I suckle for salt, and set off
on moonlit limestone paths.

Leaves quake in the wind like fish scales.
My legs keep time in bold strides.

I splash in a lake with a new friend.
In the rarefied mountain air, we race to a buoy.

I laugh as he sputters and spins in place.
He gasps for help. I tow him

a few strokes, till I can stand again.
In the man-made lake, calm, elevated,

in fresh water and transported sand,
there are bottled fears of pirates.

I have walked enough to know
there are some who do not translate

ferns to sea fans, waves to wide-eyed dreams;
some who do not see

grass drifts in rivers as it does in wind;
some who do not believe the prophecies

of the shape-shifting sea: all we pour in
returns as wind, rain, and absence.

I say, only listen: the riffle of wind on water
is the riffle of wind

on water is the riffle, the riffle....

Contraband

when we touch
    tongue
        to
    tongue
you can taste
      the languages I speak
    水 *sui* water [diphthong]

  客 *haak* guest [consonant clipped from your lips]
     sui haak 水客 water guest
  I ask you for songs
     your mother sang to you
I remember them
      and sing them in the quiet
    I know a song
  about
      a clay doll:
        她是個假娃娃
          不是個真娃娃
          她沒有親愛的媽媽
        也沒有爸爸

    泥娃娃　泥娃娃

   一個泥娃娃
        也有那鼻子也有那嘴巴
          嘴巴不說話

  ta shi ge jia wa wa   *she's a doll*
bu shi ge zhen wa wa   *not a baby*
 ta mei you tsin ai di ma ma   *she has no mommy*
ye mei you ba ba   *she has no daddy*

```
        ni wa wa     ni wa wa                    clay doll   clay doll
             yi ge ni wa wa                          a doll of clay
           ye you ge bi zi                          she has a nose
           ye you ge zui ba                        she has a mouth
          zui ba bu shuo hua                      but she can't speak
```

                    I know a song
            about a rabbit and the moon.
うさぎ うさぎ
何見て跳ねる
                        十五夜お月様
                              見て跳ねる

```
              usagi                               rabbit
                 usagi                               rabbit
           nani mite haneru                    where are you jumping to
          zyuu go ya otsuki sama              I'm jumping to the full moon
                  mite haneru                        of the fifteenth
```

when we touch
    tongue
        to
    tongue

you know
        I traffic in songs

I steal from you
    when you are not watching

    sing to you

                when you are not
        listening

                Nandito ako

umiibig sa iyo
Kahit na nagdurugo ang puso
Kung sakaling iwanan ka niya
Huwag kang mag-alala
May nagmamahal sa iyo
Nandito ako

I am here loving you
though my heart is bleeding.
If she leaves you
Don't you worry
There is someone who loves
you
I am here

I come
from a line
of smugglers

my great grandfather
was a 水客, a *water guest,*
though he walked
between
Hong Kong
and
the mainland

the contraband
--don't laugh--
dried seafood
what duty
would he have had to pay

my father arrived in the US
with a suitcase
full of nothing but ideas

US Customs and Border Protection Welcomes You to the United States
I have nothing to declare

                              my parents settled in snow
                                             snow past spring

                    I was their firstborn
                    though there was one
            before me
                              conceived
                              too early in another country
                                                       uprooted
                 from my mother's womb

Declare all articles that you have acquired abroad and are bringing into the United States.
I have nothing to declare

when we touch
       tongue
              to
       tongue
                         I taste
                    secrets like salt
                on the corner of your lips

         when your mother
                                        broke the news
                                                       of
your existence
         to your father
      he said
                         when this happens to my wife,
                           she takes care of it
               your mother did not know
                   he was married

CBP officers will determine duty.
I have nothing to declare

                        your finger
                                             travels
              along my waist
                    with no intent
         I ease you into me
                        again
                  as I would a finger into snow

Declare all articles on this declaration form and show the value in U.S. dollars.
I have nothing to declare

                        I show you
              where to find
                    the zipper on
         my raw silk blouse
                                                  as if
                                             to say
                    how would you like
              to know
                    me

when we kiss in the morning
                    you hide your tongue
                         behind your lips
I have nothing to declare

there are times travel is easy
                    as a skirt billowing around my knees
    on a bridge in Amsterdam
         a woman speaks to me in Dutch
                                        I can only guess
              she is
         asking
                                   directions
I smile and reply in the language I think we share
         I don't know

                    we laugh
                           once a year
           birds
                      build
a bridge in the sky

                              for lovers   yes
                                   also for those
                                   who laugh and say
                    I don't know.
                    不知道
                                        唔知
                         わかりません
in the Sheesh Mahal
                         mirror
                    palace
                              of Amer
                    I have seen my many selves
                              reflected
      in thousands
   of
mosaic
           mirror tiles
                                             how many selves
         have I left
behind

         once a year
      birds build a bridge in the sky

                    I travel so easily
           I could almost forget
                         how my mother refused
                                        to use
                    my US passport
      when we traveled to communist China
                if war broke

                    between
                                        the countries
                                                of my
                                                        two selves
I could claim
I don't know
je ne sais pas
I have nothing to declare

                        my father can discern
            the colors
        a crawfish sees
                                                bees see
                                        sweeps of blue
                    where we see white

                            I would like to know
        how a bee
                        regards this country
                                                    I would like to know
                what a bee
                        carries

I have (We have) commercial merchandise
(articles for sale, samples used for soliciting orders
or goods that are not considered personal effects)
I have nothing to declare

my father built a machine to parse speech
A difference profile is generated for each pair of significant phonemes by
subtracting the profile
of each phoneme from the profile of each other phoneme...

US Patent Office Abstract

he travels unquestioned across the Pacific

Controlled substances, obscene articles, and toxic substances are generally prohibited entry.
I have nothing to declare

My father quotes 莊子 Zhuang Zhi,
        who quotes Gōngsūn Lóng 公孫龍:

以指喻指之非指, 不若以非指喻指之非指也;
以馬喻馬之非馬, 不若以非馬喻馬之非馬也.
天地一指也, 萬物一馬也.

    A man approaches a border checkpoint
        with a white horse.
               The guard tells him horses are not allowed.

This is a white horse, not a horse,
      he replies.
           Confounded, the guard lets him through.

we can't apply same word *horse*
              to both
              the general class of horses
              and its subclasses
                    white horse
                    black horse
                    wild horse

yet 莊子 Zhuang Zhi concludes
萬物一馬也
the word *horse* can represent all things

I ask
does the word *American* apply
              to both

                the general class of Americans
                 and all its subclasses
                        white American
                        African American
                        Asian American
                        Native American….

can we declare
    the word *American* represents all humanity

let us keep a moment of silence
        for the
            Americans

    oscar
        grant

                                            trayvon
                                        martin
                                            jonathan
                                                ferrell
                            renisha
                                mcbride

            vincent chin
jacob valdiviezo
                                        alex nieto
                    micheal brown
                eric garner
                        freddie grey

    they are
        the unwanted children
                                of this
                                    country

        I travel so easily
            I could almost forget

                    Americans with skin of a darker hue
                        might take the subway
                            sell cigarettes
                    deliver lunch to their children
                        and never   come home

   I travel so easily
        I could almost forget

                    I am still here in this country loving you
                                        & you
                                        & you
                                        & you
                                        & you
                                   Nandito ako
                                 umiibig sa iyo
                         Kahit na nagdurugo ang puso
                        I am here loving you
                            though my heart is bleeding.

                                        broken
                                        windshields

   eggs
   thrown   into my friend's
                Honda
                                            in Ann Arbor

                    I am still here

Executive order 9066

Question #27:
Are you willing to serve in the armed forces of the United States on combat duty, wherever ordered?
Question #28: *Will you swear unqualified allegiance to the United States of America and faithfully defend the United States from any and all attack by*

*foreign or domestic forces, and forswear any form of allegiance to the
Japanese Emperor or any other foreign government, power, or organization?*

I have nothing to declare

       the 442nd Regiment
            gave themselves
             to their country
      like the rabbit
     who jumped into fire
                to feed

  an old man
  who was hungry

うさぎ うさぎ
何見てはねる
usagi usagi
nani mite haneru

            rabbit
             rabbit
        where are you jumping to

    some declared
  no no
   to
questions 27 & 28

    I will speak to you
    if you speak to me
            in a language

                  outside

   the coercion
    of forms
       and fences

                    some   danced
                        behind fences
        to the song

Oh, give me land, lots of land under starry skies
Don't fence me in
Let me ride through the wide open country that I love
Don't fence me in

some made
        love
            silently

                        tongue to tongue
                                    a tremulous
beginning

like a husky note
        in the back
    of the throat
                        an orchid stem
    with a swollen node

        a contraband
                bud

Sign on the other side of the form after you have read
this important information above and made a truthful declaration.
I have nothing to declare

                        I traffic in songs unsung
            one quiet evening
you took in a thirteen year old boy

     his song has no rainbows

only a boy doing his sums
    late
      into the evening
and a man watching him
  like the father you both imagine
          into existence

    I traffic in songs
          with quiet beginnings
  I sing them
 in the quiet
   She's a doll
    —not a baby.
     She has no loving Mama,
      no loving Papa.
   Clay doll, clay doll
    a doll of clay.
       I'll be her Mama.
       I'll be her Papa.
       I'll love her forever.

    她是個假娃娃
     不是個真娃娃
      她沒有親愛的媽媽
     也沒有爸爸

       泥娃娃　泥娃娃
      一個泥娃娃
      我做她媽媽　我做她爸爸
       永遠愛著她

The Experiment

                        i.

two monkeys   took turns
                    grooming
     a psychologist's unkempt hair:
  deft fingers
parting, searching,
        parting again

     his daughter watched
          through the small glass window
  on his office door:
                a wire grid reinforced the pane
     like an empty graph,
         experiment undone

                     ii.

...researchers reported...that rhesus monkeys refused
to pull a chain that delivered food to themselves
if doing so gave an [electric] shock to a companion.
One monkey stopped pulling the chain for twelve days
after witnessing another monkey receive a shock.
Those primates were literally starving themselves
to avoid shocking another animal.

                     iii.

dream: a protozoa flows   out
     of an open square
                        four lines   three corners
                      & a gap

    for escape
          from the Euclidean

iv.

salt   through the placenta
           down the gradient

$\frac{dy}{dx}$ $\lim_{x \to 0}$
        stillframe
          the smallest increment of change
    diffuse

there was   a time and place   when
      laws forbade
    gathering salt from the sea

        each grain gathered
           placed   on the tongue
        went down
            the salinity slope
    in
      & out

$\frac{dy}{dx}$
the smallest   increment of change
    diffuse
  in the Salt Satyagraha

there is no prisoner's dilemma
  no wall
      between prisoners
when the conscience volunteers

    in
    & out

v.

           there are   an infinite
   number of   possible
                        curves
             through discrete points:
plot one
  of love.

The Way of Knots

                i.

This lace fastens a child's shoe:
bights tighten, then flourish.

This ribbon joins two wreaths
on the heads of a new couple.

This knot neither slips nor jams
as it glides in a rescuer's hands.

This cord, severed at birth,
leaves a painless scar on the belly.

                ii.

The back stitch takes one step back and two steps forward.
It holds on to its gains.

                iii.

In a running stitch, only half the stitches are visible on each face of the cloth.

Somewhere, there is an anteater shuffling among rotting leaves.

If I am content to look out the window at the oblique sun,
there will be room for us both: me and the anteater.

                iv.

A child unwinds a clue of yarn.
Unschooled in the art of measure,
she lets it roll.

A child makes a path for herself in the Himalayan snow.

The wind erases her footprints. She has left her parents
to walk towards a school where her language is not forbidden.

A child cannot sleep. He looks out the window at other lights in the darkness, as
if each were a glimmer of story.

Gloved hands untie the body's gift in helical ribbons.

A bumper sticker on a car: "Why, if not for love?"

These could be five stories, more, or one.

v.

Do a search on the web. Each node is an invisible hand.

vi.

A line of dancers, hand in hand, form a fence.
The dancer at the head passes under
the raised arms of two dancers at the tail;
the fence admits itself, once and again,
till it's wound tight, and the only movement
it permits is to unwind itself in reverse,
so the dancers, hand in hand, form a fence,
then let go, and each is free to roam again.

vii.

Bind a journal with needle and thread.
Promise to remember.

A buttonhole stitch guards against fraying, for now.

A running stitch without knots passes through
and leaves nothing but a line of holes.

Notes

Trade Winds is based on a 19th century sculpture from Canton, China.

California Rain Song
Quotes from *The Emeryville Shellmound* by Max Uhle, University of California Publications 1910, and *Bay Nature*, July-Sept 2005.

After Hours at the Convent School and **Staircase**
A number of schools in Hong Kong were occupied by the Japanese army between 1941 and 1945.

Acknowledgments

Bamboo Ridge: "After Hours at the Convent School", "Staircase"

Blue Collar Review: "10,000 Thumbs"

Blue Lyra Review: "A Day in British Hong Kong", "Mother"

California Quarterly: "Flotsam", "Letter from Sister to Brother", "Where Indigo Meets Azure", "Wishbone", "Brooding", "A Portrait of Winds (excerpts)", "The Taste of Each (excerpt)"

The Columbia Review: "Landing", "The Boots and the Weary Bird"

Crab Orchard Review: "Sisters"

Contemporary Verse 2 (Canada): "GI Bill", "Quotidian"

Drunken Boat: "Fore and Aft"

Earth's Daughters: "The Journey of Goods"

Families: the Frontline of Pluralism: "Common Flower", "To Swim Daily"

The Pedestal: "The Reader"

Nimrod: "Warp and Weft", "California Rain Song"

Runes: "The Parting of Hair," "House of Paper"

sparkle and blink: "Contraband"

Spillways: "The Work of Knots", "Open Circles", "Cartographies"

Taos Journal of International Poetry and Art: "The Tale"

Turning a Train of Thought Upside Down: "Common Flower", "To Unborn Sons" (reprints)

Yellow As Turmeric, Fragrant As Cloves: "Letter to Unborn Sons", "All that She Wants"

About the Author

Bonnie Wai-Lee Kwong is a poet and software developer in the San Francisco Bay Area. She has lived in nine states and two continents. Writing is a way for her to traverse seen and unseen geographies. She speaks Cantonese, Mandarin, some Japanese, English, ruby, and javascript.

Kwong's poetry has been nominated for two Pushcart Prizes. Among her projects is a digital anthology, *The Taste of Each*, curated around references to oranges and bananas in various literary and artistic works across the world.

Kwong's first poetry collection, *ravel*, spans wide and invites readers to interrogate boundaries. It has been listed as a finalist for the Many Voices Project by New Rivers Press, and the White Pine Press Poetry Prize. The digital index page for *ravel* can be accessed at www.bonniekwong.info/ravel.

photograph by Bob Hsiang

NeoPoiesis: *a new way of making*

1) in ancient Greece, poiesis referred to the process of making: creation - production - organization - formation - causation

2) a process that can be physical and spiritual, biological and intellectual, artistic and technological, material and teleological, efficient and formal

3) a means of modifying the environment and a method of organizing the self, the making of art and music and poetry, the fashioning of memory and history and philosophy, the construction of perception and expression and reality

4) an independent publisher with a steadfast goal to print and promote outstanding poets, writers and artists that reflect the creative drive and spirit of the new electronic landscape

NeoPoiesisPress.com

www.ingramcontent.com/pod-product-compliance
Lightning Source LLC
Chambersburg PA
CBHW022001100426
42738CB00042B/1173